Cultural Celebrations

DiscoverRoo
An Imprint of Pop!
popbooksonline.com

HANUKKAH

by Elizabeth Andrews

WELCOME TO DiscoverRoo!

This book is filled with videos, puzzles, games, and more! Scan the QR codes* while you read, or visit the website below to make this book pop.

popbooksonline.com/hanukkah

abdobooks.com
Published by Pop!, a division of ABDO, PO Box 398166, Minneapolis, Minnesota 55439.

Printed in the United States of America, North Mankato, Minnesota.

102023
012024

THIS BOOK CONTAINS RECYCLED MATERIALS

Cover: Getty Images

Interior: Shutterstock Images; Getty Images; José Luiz Bernardes Ribeiro/Antiochus IV Epiphanes - Altes Museum; Wikimedia

Editor: Emily Dreher

Series Designer: Colleen McLaren

Library of Congress Control Number: 2023939065

Publisher's Cataloging-in-Publication Data

Names: Andrews, Elizabeth, author.

Title: Hanukkah / by Elizabeth Andrews

Description: Minneapolis, Minnesota : Pop!, 2024 | Series: Cultural celebrations | Includes online resources and index

Identifiers: ISBN 9781098245382 (lib. bdg.) | ISBN 9781098245948 (ebook)

Subjects: LCSH: Hanukkah--Juvenile literature. | Feast of Lights--Juvenile literature. | Fasts and feasts--Judaism--Juvenile literature. | Holidays--Juvenile literature. | Cultural sociology--Juvenile literature.

Classification: DDC 394.26--dc23

*Scanning QR codes requires a web-enabled smart device with a QR code reader app and a camera.

TABLE OF CONTENTS

CHAPTER 1

LIGHTS AND LATKES

It is a cold winter afternoon outside, and Joe's home fills with the sound of sizzling. He and his family are cooking latkes for the family dinner tonight. Joe helps form the potato mixture into patties before his mom sets them in the oil to fry.

WATCH A VIDEO HERE!

Latkes are made of potatoes, flour, onions, eggs, and seasonings.

Some Jewish people only eat kosher foods. These are foods that fit Jewish dietary rules.

Today is the final night of Hanukkah. Joe is Jewish, and he loves this time of year. He gets to see family, play games, and eat delicious food. After he's done helping with the latkes, he goes out and sets the table. By his dad's plate, he places the menorah.

DID YOU KNOW?

Some people dip latkes in applesauce or sour cream.

Joe's extended family arrive a few minutes before the sun goes down. Everyone gathers around the table to listen to his grandpa say blessings. Then his father lights eight candles on the menorah. Joe and his family sing. The lit menorah is moved to glow in the window. It's finally time to eat!

Songs are often sung in the traditional Jewish language called Hebrew.

CHAPTER 2

HISTORY OF HANUKKAH

Hanukkah celebrates an important moment in Jewish history. The ancient Jewish people **settled** in a city called Jerusalem. They built the Temple of Jerusalem to contain the most **revered** Jewish items. All the Jewish people visited the temple for **rituals**.

LEARN MORE HERE!

One item kept in the temple was called the Ark of the Covenant.

The Second Temple of Jerusalem was less grand than the First.

Enemies of the Jewish people destroyed the Temple of Jerusalem. The enemies kicked the Jews out of their home. Less than 100 years later, Jewish people returned and built the Second Temple of Jerusalem. It was home to Jewish **worship** for nearly 350 years.

In 169 BCE, the Syrian ruler Antiochus IV took over the Temple. He ordered the Jews to pray to the Greek gods and give up their religion. But they refused. Antiochus IV put statues of Greek gods inside the Temple. The act was very disrespectful to Jewish people.

Antiochus IV liked Greek culture and fought to spread it around the world.

A group of Jewish soldiers fought the Syrians and won the Temple back. Judas Maccabaeus led the very skilled army. When they entered the temple, they **purified** it and **dedicated** it back to their God. Judas protected the Jewish faith.

Soldiers used swords and spears to fight battles.

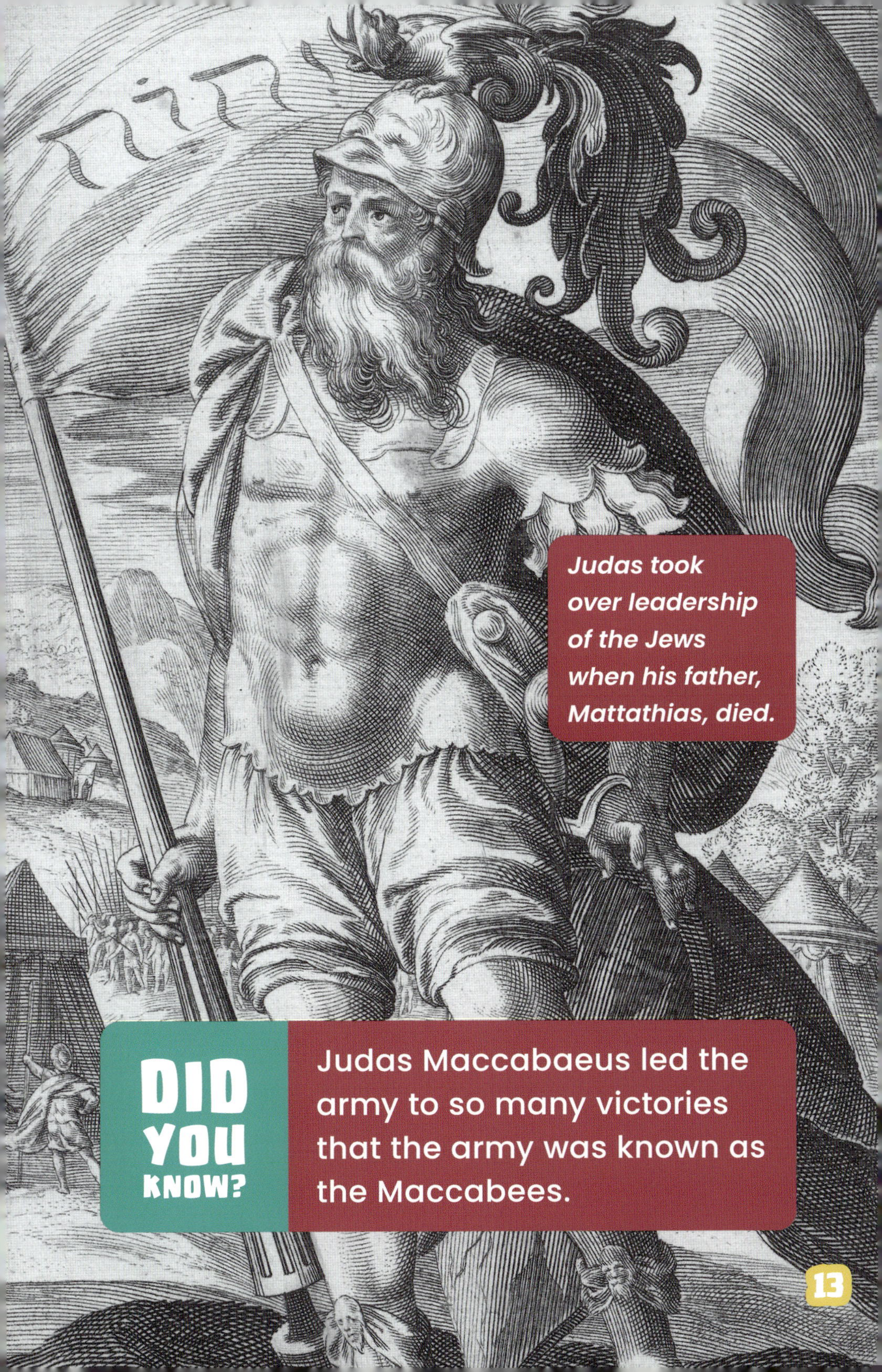

Judas took over leadership of the Jews when his father, Mattathias, died.

DID YOU KNOW?

Judas Maccabaeus led the army to so many victories that the army was known as the Maccabees.

Menorahs can be large and elaborately decorated.

During the rededication, the Maccabees needed oil to light a large menorah. They found enough oil for only one day. But the menorah **miraculously** stayed lit for eight days. Judas ordered Jews to hold an eight-day celebration in honor of the victory every year. This yearly celebration became known as Hanukkah.

JEWISH RESILIENCE

Resilience means an ability to recover from misfortune. Jewish people have faced hardships since the beginning of the religion. They have been enslaved and forced out of their homes. During the **Holocaust** more than six million Jews were killed by the Nazis. Jewish people are proud of their ability to survive such violence.

CHAPTER 3

HANUKKAH TRADITIONS

Hanukkah lasts eight days. The exact dates of Hanukkah change from year to year. Instead of following the traditional calendar used by much of the world, Hanukkah follows the Hebrew calendar.

EXPLORE LINKS HERE!

It begins on the 25th day of the month of Kislev. This is the same day the Second Temple was won back.

The number of days in a Hebrew calendar's year can range from 353 to 385 days.

The menorah is the **symbol** of Hanukkah. It is a lamp also known as hanukiah. Most menorahs hold nine candles. There is one candle to

Some menorahs used today are still lit using oil.

represent each night the oil lasted for the Maccabees. There is an extra candle to use for lighting. This ninth candle is called the shammash.

The menorah is lit at sunset on each night of Hanukkah. Using the shammash, candles are lit from left to right. On the first night, one candle is placed and lit. On the second night, another candle is added and lit. The pattern continues over all eight nights. Often, lit menorahs are set in windows to share their light with the community.

Menorah candles are left lit until they burn out.

The Torah is part of a group of books that make up the Hebrew Bible.

After adding the correct number of candles for each night, blessings are said before the lighting. The blessings may be scripture or prayers from the Torah. Families may sing hymns too.

DID YOU KNOW?

Olive oil was used to light the menorah before candles became the tradition.

HOW TO PLAY DREIDEL

Rules:

- Players sit in a circle with 10 to 15 tokens each. Tokens can be chocolate coins, pennies, or other small objects.
- Each player puts two tokens in the center. This is the pot.
- Youngest player spins the dreidel first.
- Follow steps according to what letter lands facing up.
- Players lose by running out of tokens.
- Last player with tokens wins!

Gimel: Get
Take everything from the pot. Other players add two tokens to make new pot.

Nun: Nothing
Take no tokens.

Hey: Half
Take half of the pot. If there is an odd number of tokens in the pot, decide as a group what to do.

Shin: Share
Add two tokens to the pot.

Hanukkah celebrates the strength and **perseverance** of Jewish people. Some families fill their homes with lights and blue and white decorations.

People give gifts during Hanukkah. Kids sometimes receive money or chocolate gold coins. Children also play the traditional Hanukkah game dreidel.

Chocolate gold coins represent the traditional Jewish gelt.

CHAPTER 4

HANUKKAH AROUND THE WORLD

A special part of Hanukkah is the food. Jewish people make fried foods of all kinds to honor the **miraculous** oil that burned for eight days. Latkes are potato

COMPLETE AN ACTIVITY HERE!

Challah is a Jewish braided bread. People eat it on special holidays.

pancakes fried in oil. A classic dessert is the fried, jelly-filled donut called *sufganiyah*. Jewish people eat different treats all around the world.

A large Hanukkah menorah is put up next to a Christmas tree in Berlin, Germany.

Israel is home to the most Jewish people in one country. Hanukkah is widely celebrated there. Schools are closed, and giant menorahs are displayed on important buildings. Neighborhoods glow every night from menorahs in windows. Some homes even have cutouts in their outdoor walls to place menorahs.

DID YOU KNOW?

Morocco, Algeria, and some places in India also display their menorahs outside during Hanukkah.

Some North African Jews spend one day of Hanukkah celebrating the women in Jewish history who protected their faith. One woman was named Judith. She killed a war leader named Holofernes during the struggle to take back the Second Temple. Judith got close enough to kill Holofernes by offering him cheese. Now, Jews all around the world eat cheese during Hanukkah to celebrate her.

Many famous works of art feature Judith.

Hanukkah celebrations in Budapest, Hungary, have become large and popular. The Jewish community in Hungary has faced many hardships. Now, they can publicly celebrate holidays such as Hanukkah. There are neighborhood menorah lightings on streets decorated with lights.

Many Jewish religious leaders called rabbis ice skate during Hanukkah in Budapest.

During Hanukkah, Jewish people feel proud of everything their faith has survived.

Jewish people have struggled through much of their history. Many groups of people tried to force them to give up their faith, but they **persevered**. Hanukkah is a chance for Jews all over the world to celebrate all their victories.

MAKING CONNECTIONS

TEXT-TO-SELF

What part of Hanukkah celebrations were you most interested in? Please explain your answer.

TEXT-TO-TEXT

Have you read any books about other Jewish holidays? If so, what did those holidays have in common with Hanukkah?

TEXT-TO-WORLD

Much of Jewish history is filled with hard times. Jewish people enjoy celebrating the perseverance of their faith. Can you think of any other groups of people who have faced hard times? How do they celebrate their own perseverance?

GLOSSARY

dedicate — to set aside something for a sacred or serious purpose.

Holocaust — the killing of millions of Jewish people and others by Nazi Germany during World War II.

miraculous — highly unusual and unexpected that happens because of a holy power.

perseverance — (*noun*) the quality that allows a person to keep trying to do something even though it is difficult. To persevere is to keep going when things are challenging.

purify — to free of undesirable elements.

revere — to regard something as a great honor.

ritual — a religious action performed in a certain way.

settle — to build a place to live.

symbol — something that stands for something else.

worship — love, respect, and affection shown to God.

INDEX